For Judy
Bear Hug,
Stephski 2
'97

TEDDY BEARS
Images of Love

by Ho Phi Le

A journey into a human's heart...

Especially for...
Susan Wiley
Anna Taccino
Mary Beth Ruddell
Linda & Wally Mullins
Little Darlings at Adelaide Elementary
and
Those who love teddy bears

Additional copies of this book may be purchased at $16.95 (plus postage and handling) from
Hobby House Press, Inc.
1 Corporate Drive
Grantsville, Maryland 21536
1-800-554-1447
or from your favorite bookstore or dealer.

©1997 Ho Phi Le

All rights reserved. No part of this book may be reproduced or utilized in any form or by any means, electronic or mechanical, including photocopying, recording, or by any information storage and retrieval system, without permission in writing from the publisher. Inquiries should be addressed to
Hobby House Press, Inc., 1 Corporate Drive, Grantsville, Maryland 21536.
Printed in the United States of America

ISBN: 0-87588-498-9

Images of Love

Do you remember the feeling of tenderness
when you hold in your arms the teddy bear
of your childhood?
Do you feel the love
from a friend of years long past?
Do you know that Teddy Bear is
forever a part of your life,
for he brings so much heart
in moments of loneliness?
When all else fails, Teddy Bear will
always be there to comfort and soothe your soul.
Please don't ever stop believing
in the goodness of your teddy bear
because he's the symbol of love and happiness.

To celebrate our love
for the most beloved creature of them all,
I have captured here beautiful images
that come straight from my heart & soul.

Ho Phi Le

Waiting for the morning light
to softly come,
I think of you.

A day full of memories,   A day full of love,

A day full of happiness,   A day to remember.

Do you see the reflection
of our images
in the river of our dream?
Do you feel the love
that I have
for you and only you?
Do you know
what is in my heart,
my son,
my dearest one?

Ho Phi Le

By the river,
you taught me
how to fish,
By the river,
I caught
my very first fish,
By the river,
we shared a moment of
gentleness,
By the river,
a special gift
had just been given
from a father
to his son,
By the river,
how could I forget.

Ho Phi Le

O, childhood,
O, my childhood,
Days of heaven
Under the silvery clouds,
Filled with sunshine
In the bluest sky,
Chasing dreams
in the moonlit night,
Watching seasons
Swiftly going by.

Ho Phi Le

I love you, Teddy,
Because you are in my heart,
I love you, Teddy
Because you are in my soul,
I love you for today,
I love you for tomorrow,
I love you for always.

Ho Phi Le

I love teddy bears
because they are so personable.

Barbara Lauver

His face steals my heart!
He is a very special companion
with his arms outstretched ready
to love unconditionally.
The world could learn much from
this fuzzy little character.

Steve Estes

Teddy and Bunny are so funny,
Teddy and Bunny sure love honey,
Teddy and Bunny are so furry,
Teddy and Bunny are in a hurry.

Nichole Atkinson & Kelly Cunningham

I love teddy bears
because my wife loves them.
What ever makes her happy,
makes me happy.
Teddy bears keep everything
in harmony with the marriage.

Wally Mullins

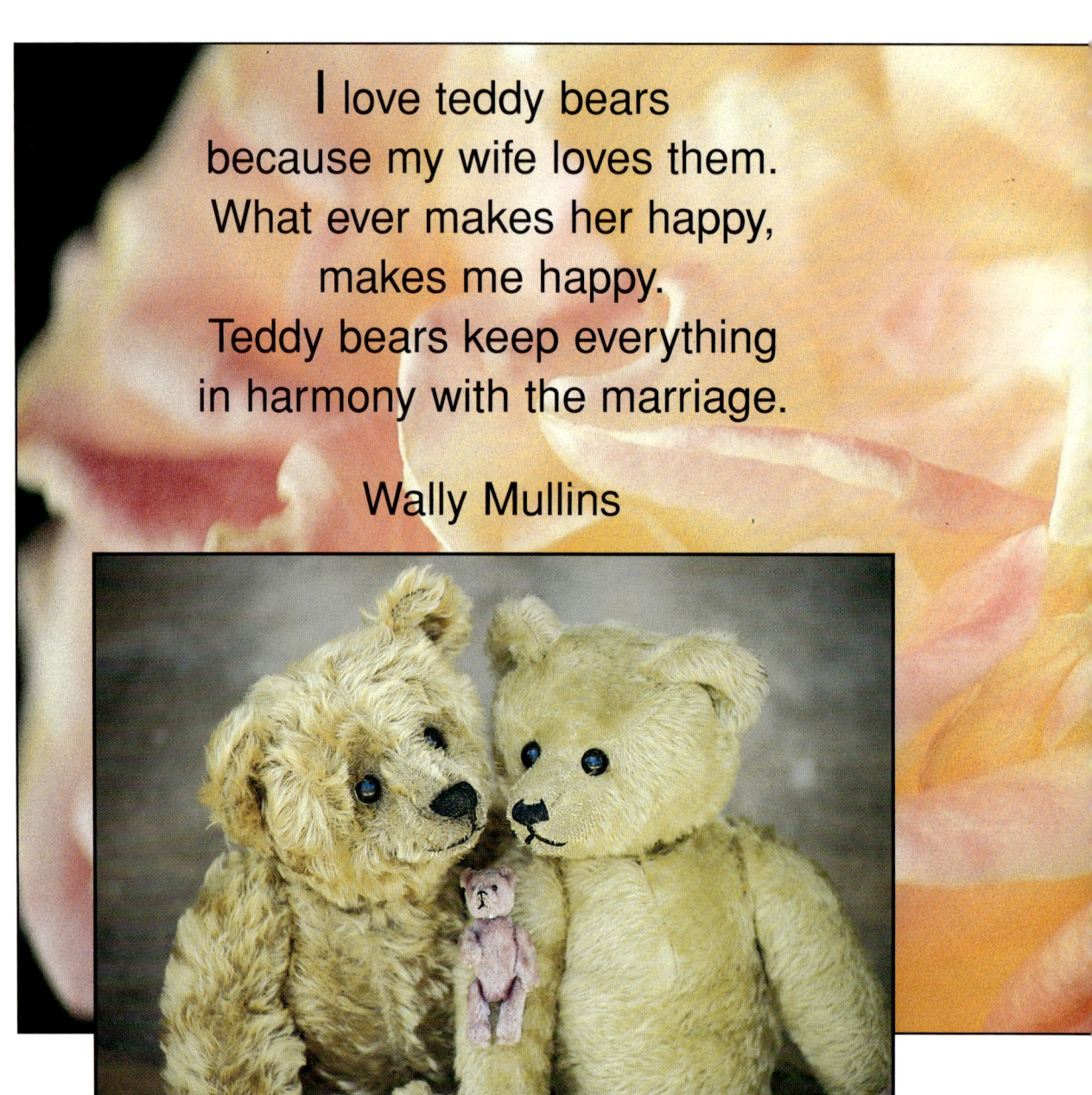

Teddy bear has
a magical power on people.
I can't imagine
the world
without
teddy bears.

Linda Mullins

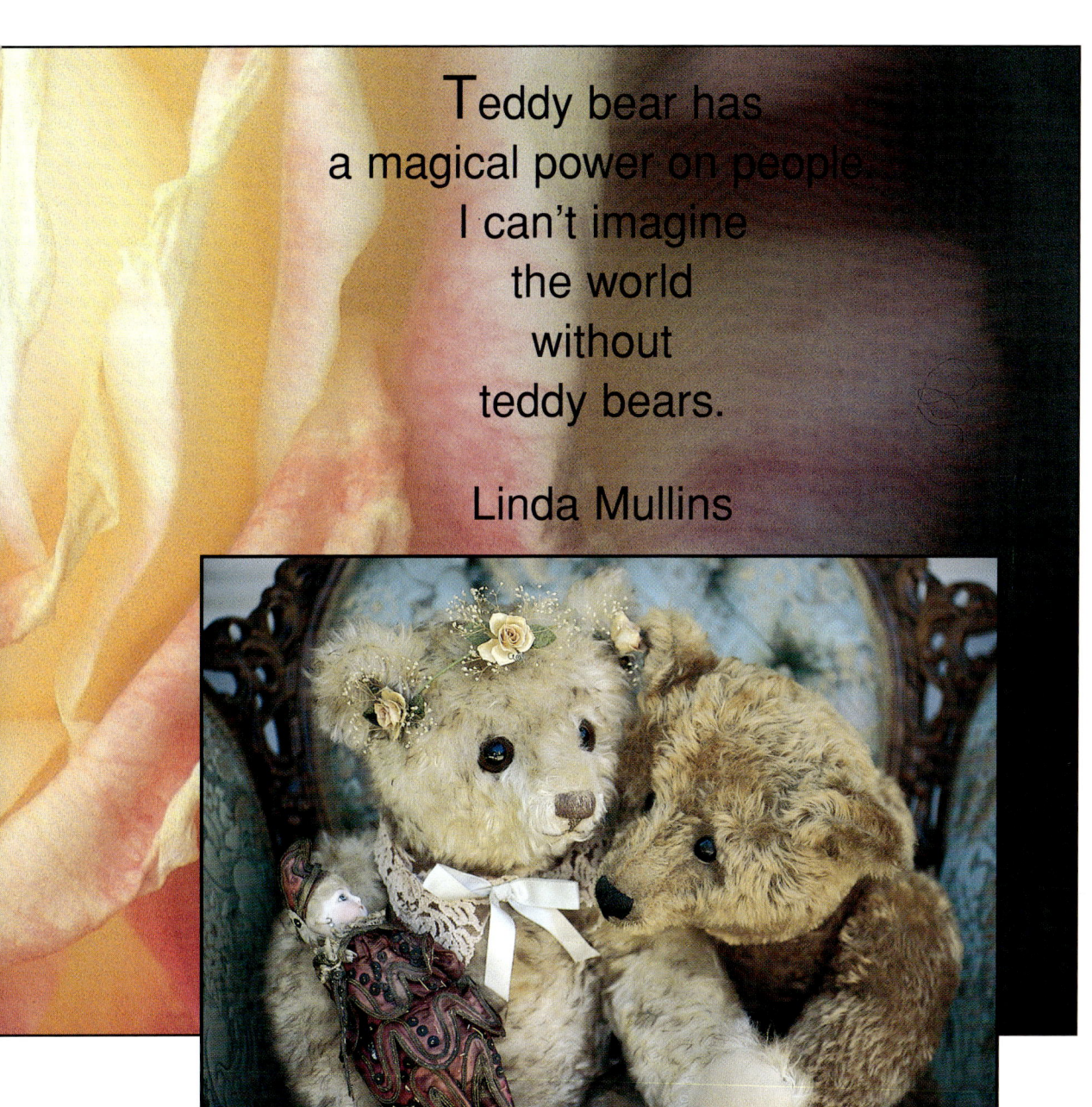

What looks at me,
With round wet eyes,
And never says a word,
Yet deep down in your heart,
You know it can be heard?

What's large round and plump,
With shimmering fur that glows?
And when you are sad and gloomy,
Its love really showed?

Even when you get him dirty,
He doesn't really care,
So what could it be?
But a big, cuddly Teddy Bear!

Eva Young

Once I had a teddy bear,
And his fur was soft and nice.
He always wore a smile
On that bright little face of his.
He liked me, and I liked him.
But one day when we were on a walk,
He met another teddy.
They fell in love,
And now I have two teddies
Whom I love so dearly.

Sara Fey

Goorangi
loves his teddies.
He's always
staying near.
He teaches them
to hunt and to share
the fun with
the beating drum.
Goorangi loves
his teddies.

Jonathan Lee

My black teddy is
soft and fluffy,
I cuddle him up
so close to me,
People think
my black teddy is scary,
But he is not
really,
I love him more
than my heart can bear.

Steven McLain

A Teddy Bear is like
an angel of peace,
that will be friends with you
forever and ever.

Jessica Baldwin

Do you love me
no matter what?

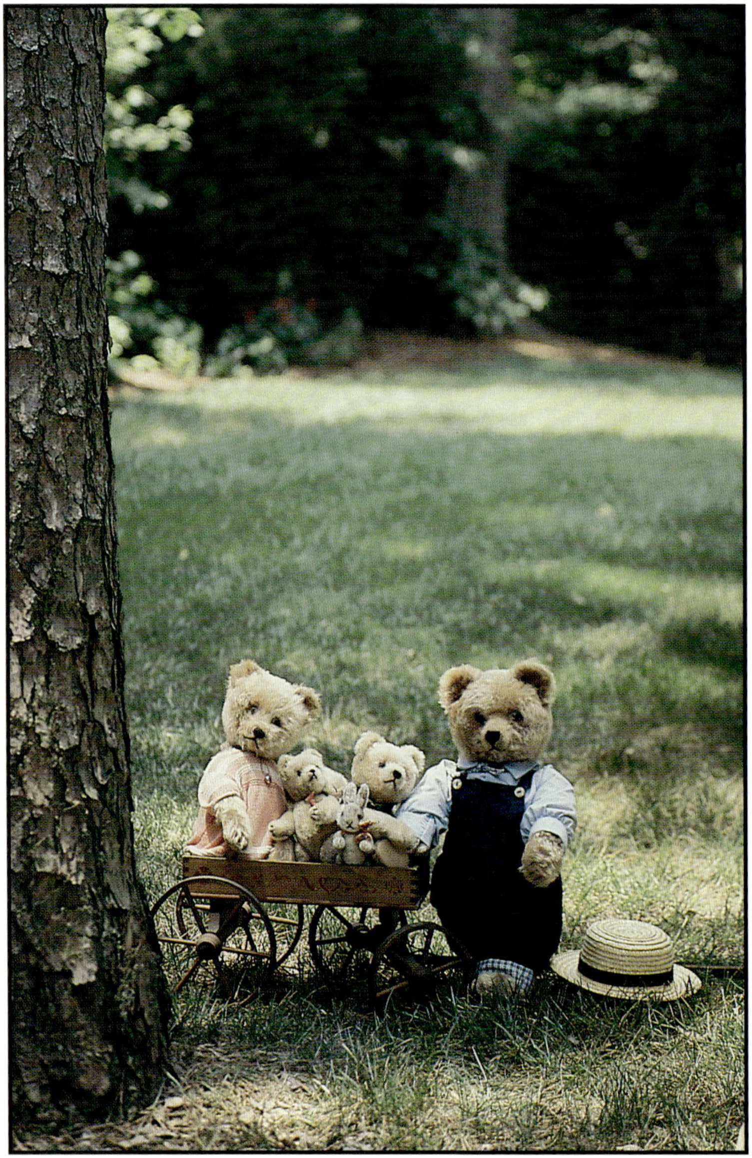

I have many teddy bears,
That are cute, furry, and warm.
But my favorite one
Is the one I got first,
Which is tattered, battered, and worn.

I am not saying that my other bears
Don't mean a lot, you see.
But my dearest one
Is my oldest one
That really cares about me.

Eva Young

Teddy Bear's filled with love,
Made with silver and golden fur.

Crystal Anderson

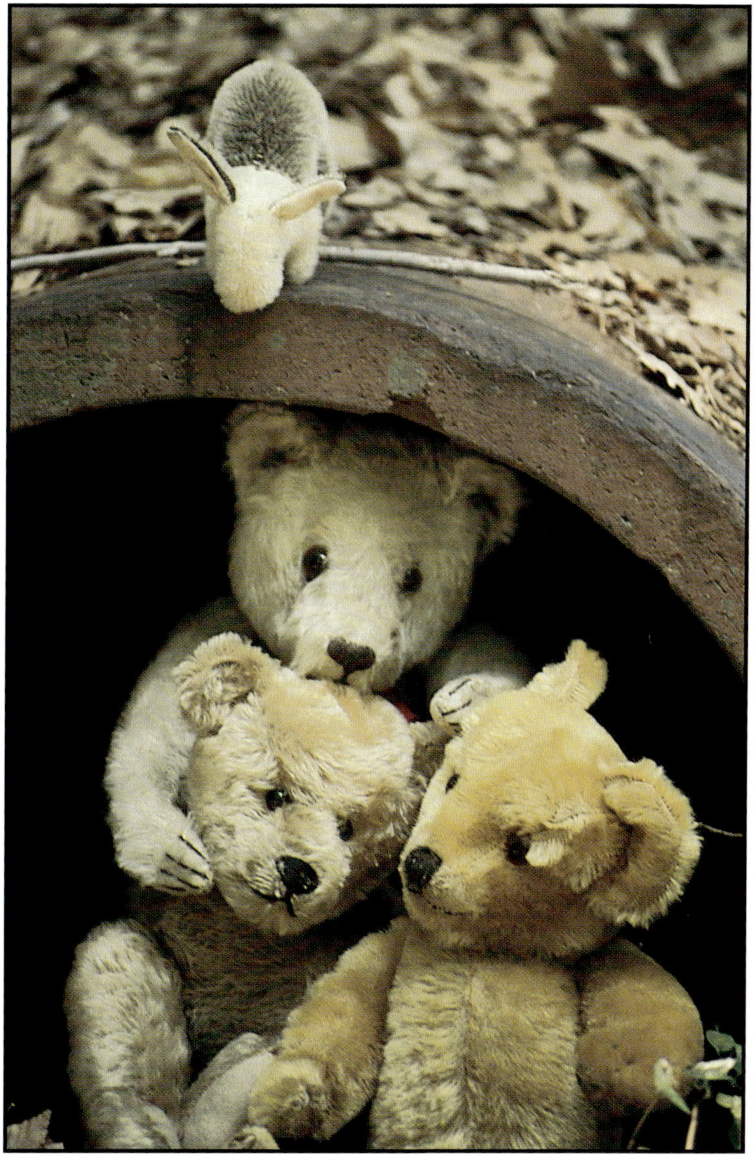

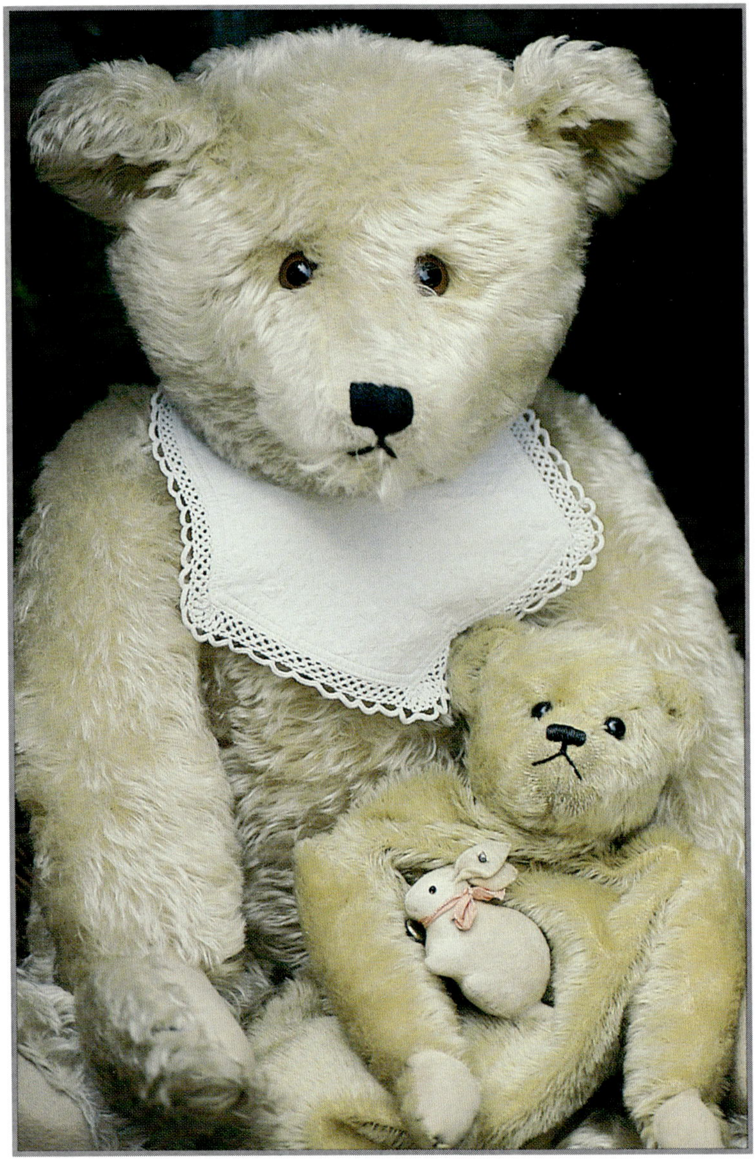

Oh, Teddy, Oh, Teddy,
You're as white as a snow,
You're as beautiful as a bow,
You hop like a bunny,
That's why I call you Sunny.

Korina Rodriguez

I love to hug,
I love to snug,
All nights...
All days...
I just want to say
I love you,
Teddy.

Slavik Denchik

I have
only
one teddy
and
I am glad
that he loves me.

Norma Morales

My teddy bear is small and brown,
he can move his arms and legs around,
he has pretty soft hair,
and he looks exactly like a baby bear.

Emily Musick

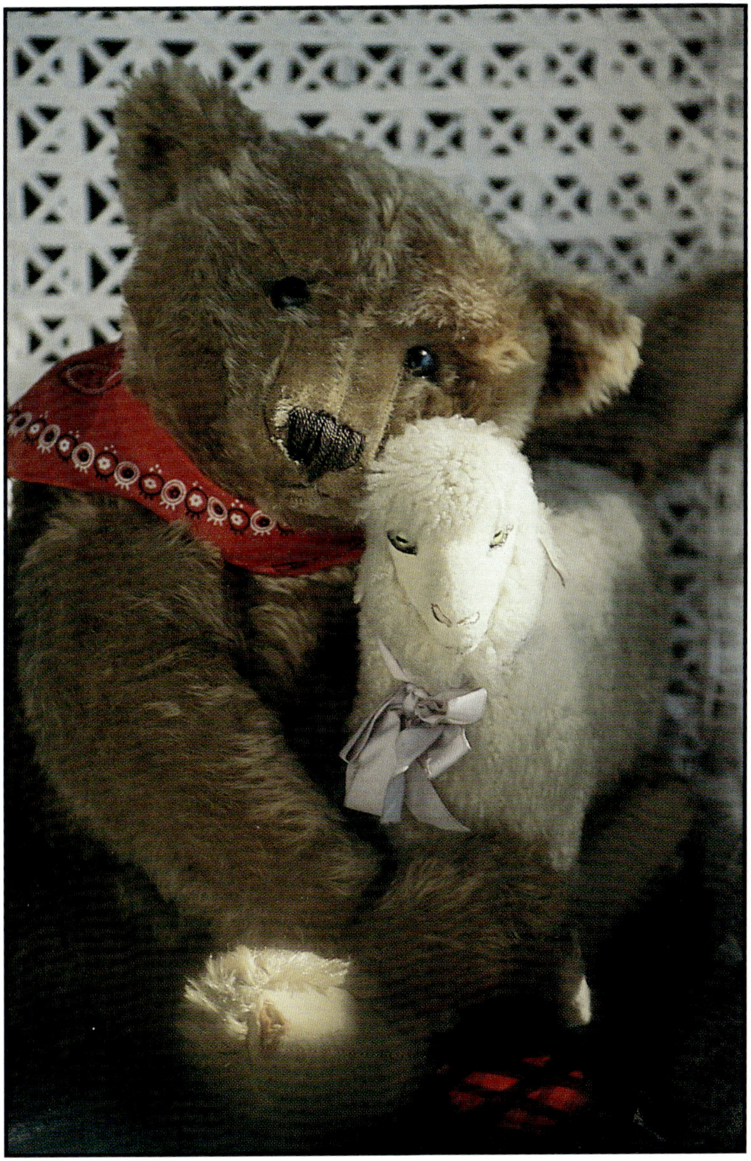

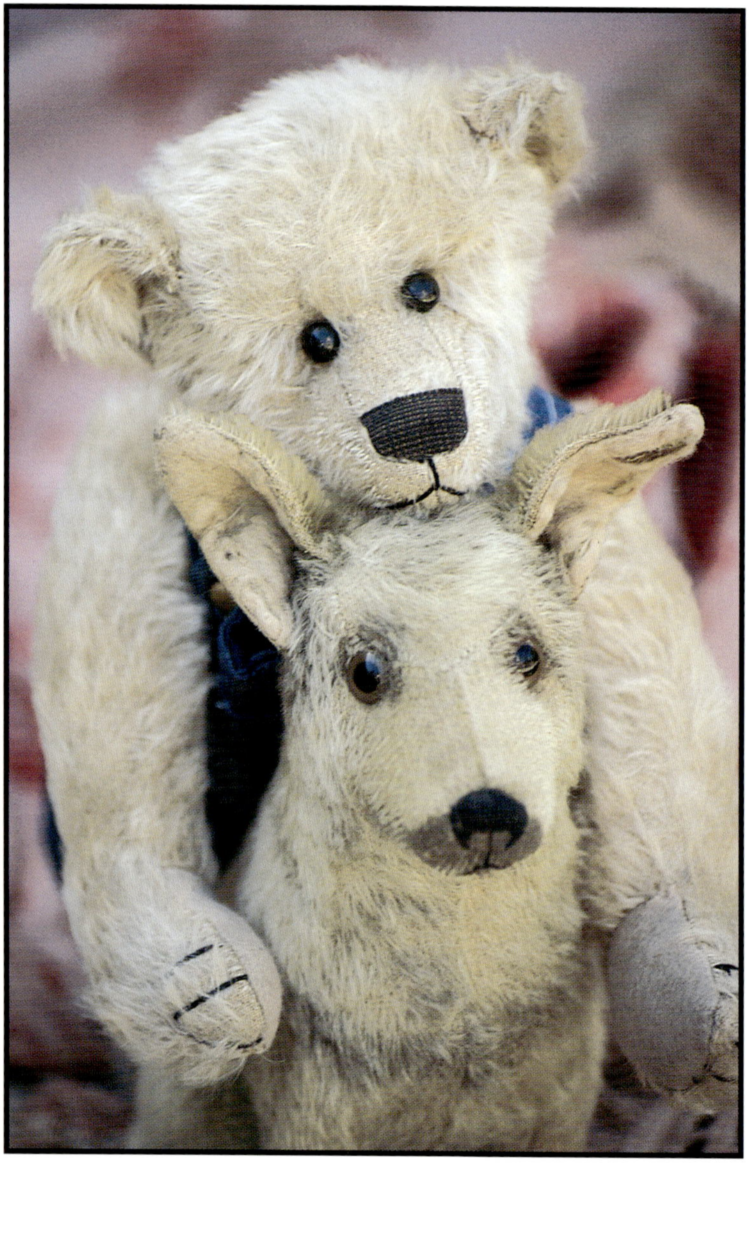

My teddy bear
is loud,
And he likes
To smell the ground.
He also likes
To pound on my hound,
And my hound likes
To pound on him.

Kevin Day

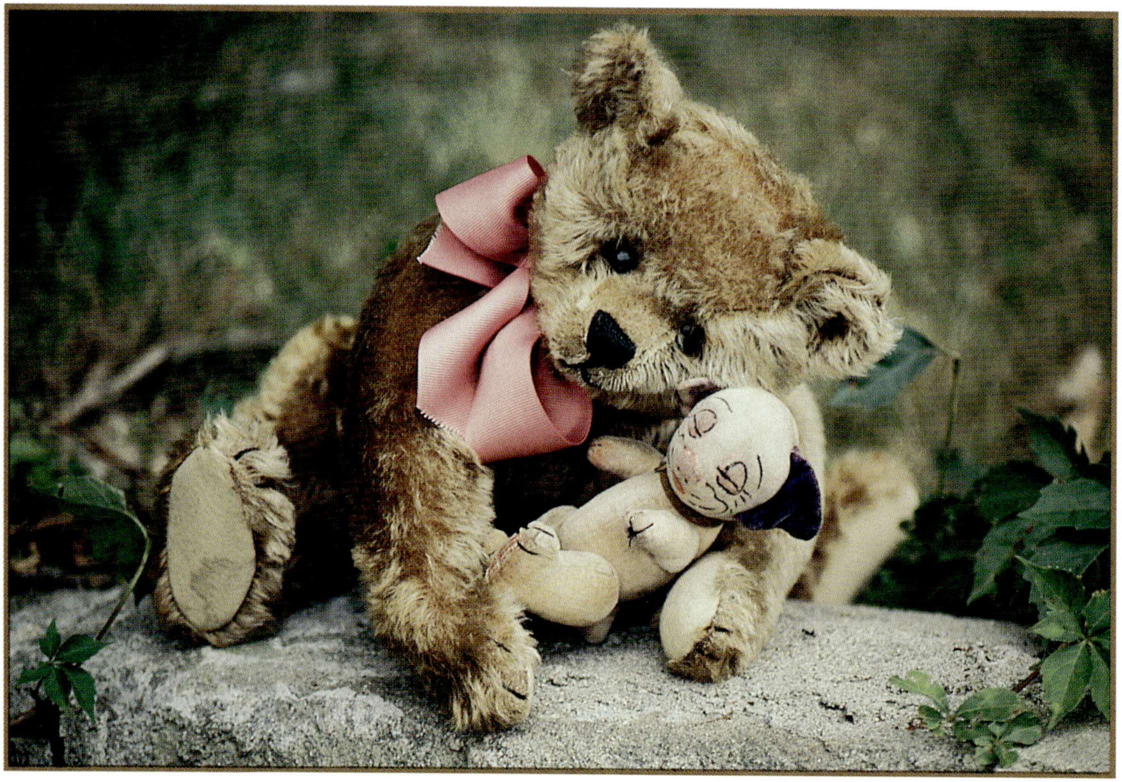

My teddy bear was once not loved.
My teddy bear always got shoved.
My teddy bear was once treated like dirt.
The people who owned him ripped up his shirt.
One Sunday I found him in the trash.
On his head there was a bad gash.
That Sunday I rescued him.
The people who owned him had really sinned.
Now today my teddy bear is loved.
Now my teddy bear won't get shoved.

Gabe Conant

Where is my teddy?
Where might my teddy be?
Then I saw him
on some golden soft hair,
And he said, "Look at me! Look at me!"
Oh, teddy, you're so naughty!

Amanda Richardson

Teddy Bear, White Sheep,
hiding everywhere,
looking, peeking, up, down,
even upside down,
Teddy Bear, White Sheep,
bear hugs, sheep hugs,
Baa--aa--aa!

Jeff Lim

A teddy is like a flower
On a sunny summer day.
You'd pick him in a minute
If you could have your way.
A teddy is like the sunshine,
He warms your heart each day.
He makes you feel like smiling,
It's just his special way
Of saying that he loves you,
The way that teddies do.
A teddy is very special.
That's the way I love him too.

Stephanie Niner

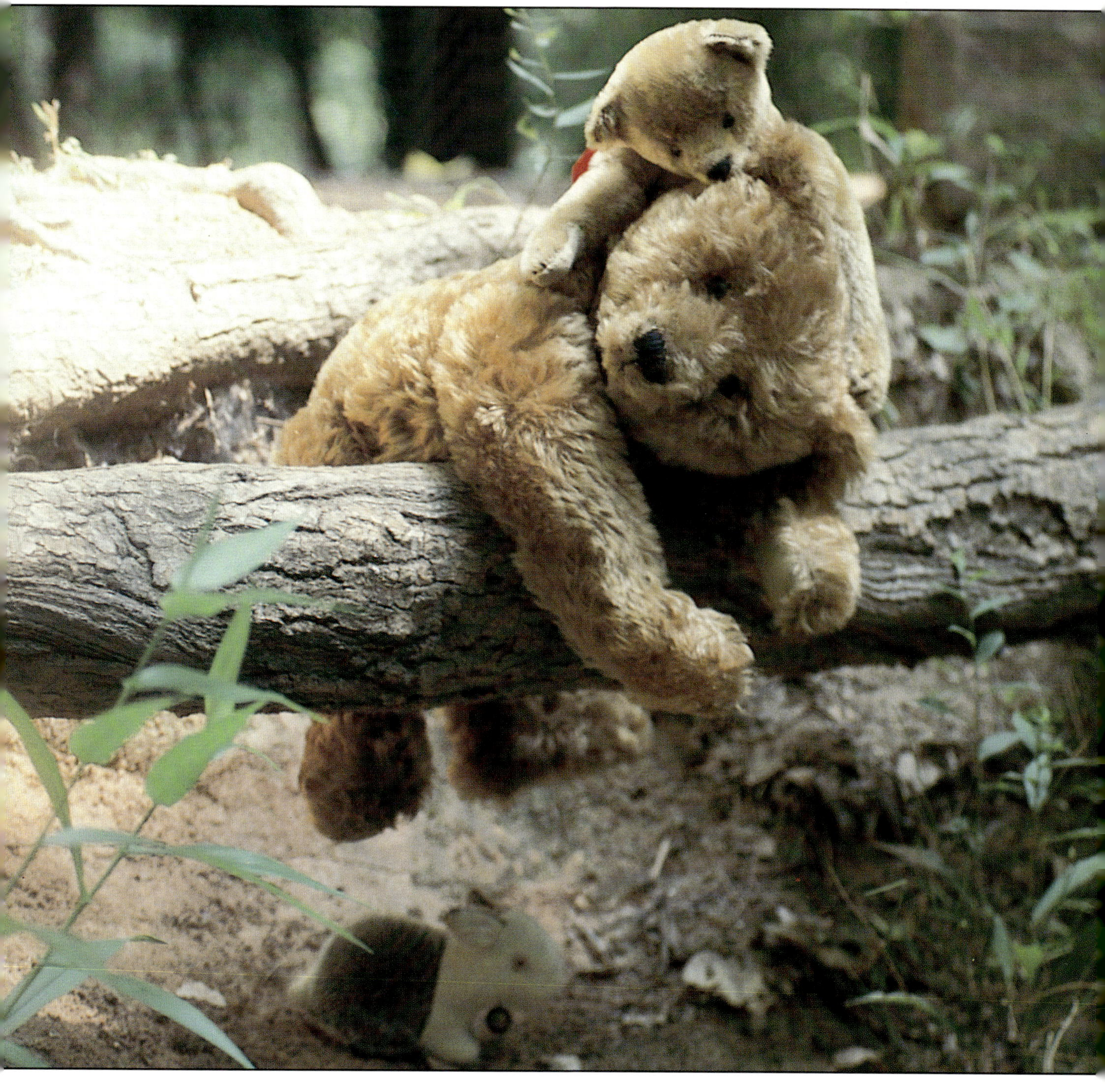

When I am with my teddy,
There is a special glow in my heart,
Nothing else can make my heart glow,
But being with her.

Kelly Leach

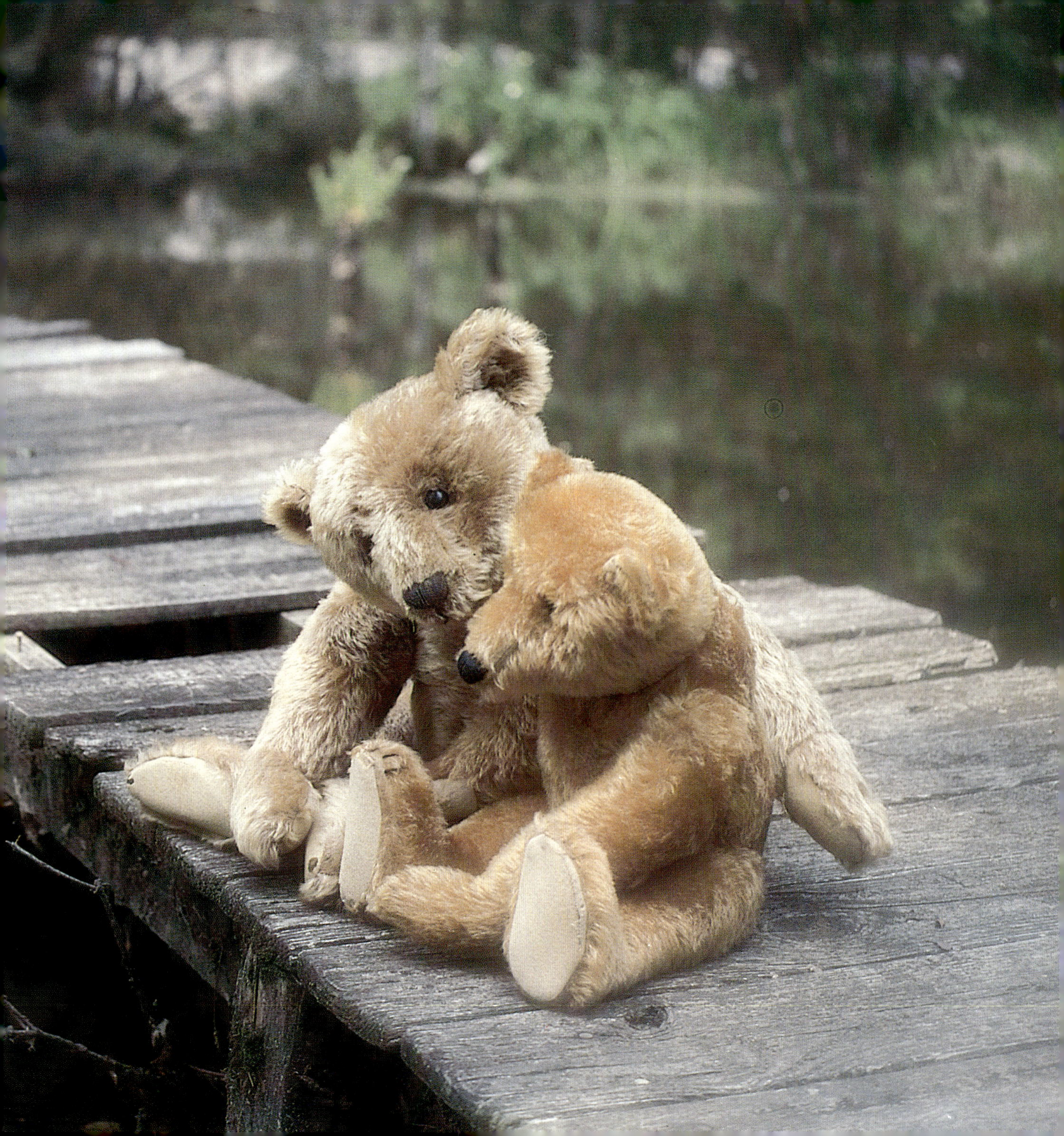

When I was a little boy,
I didn't know how to swim
in the river of my dream.
So I let a dragonfly
bite my belly button,
believing that I could swim
with ease.
I did that once upon a river,
and a swimmer I was not...
even now or even then.

Ho Phi Le

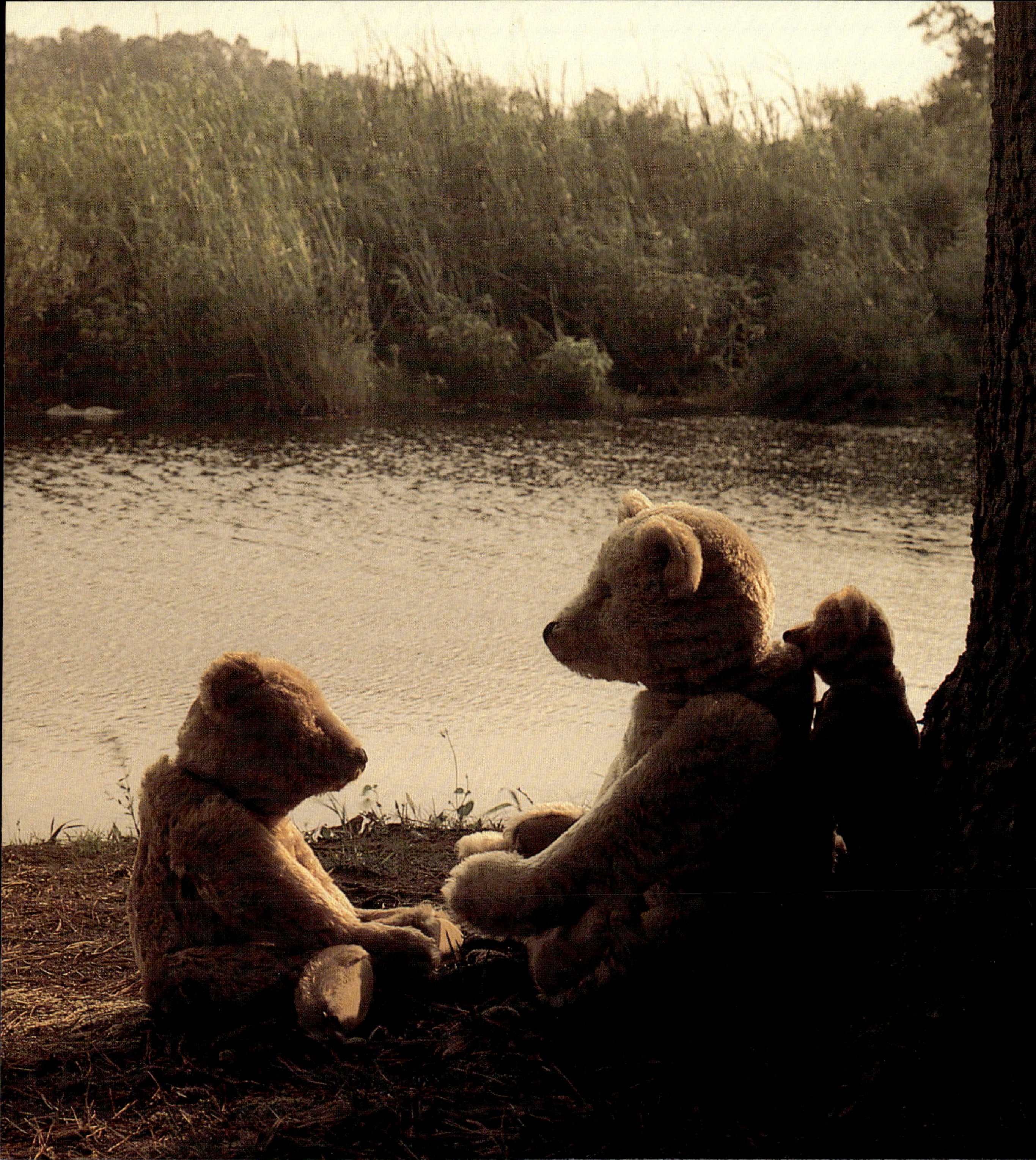

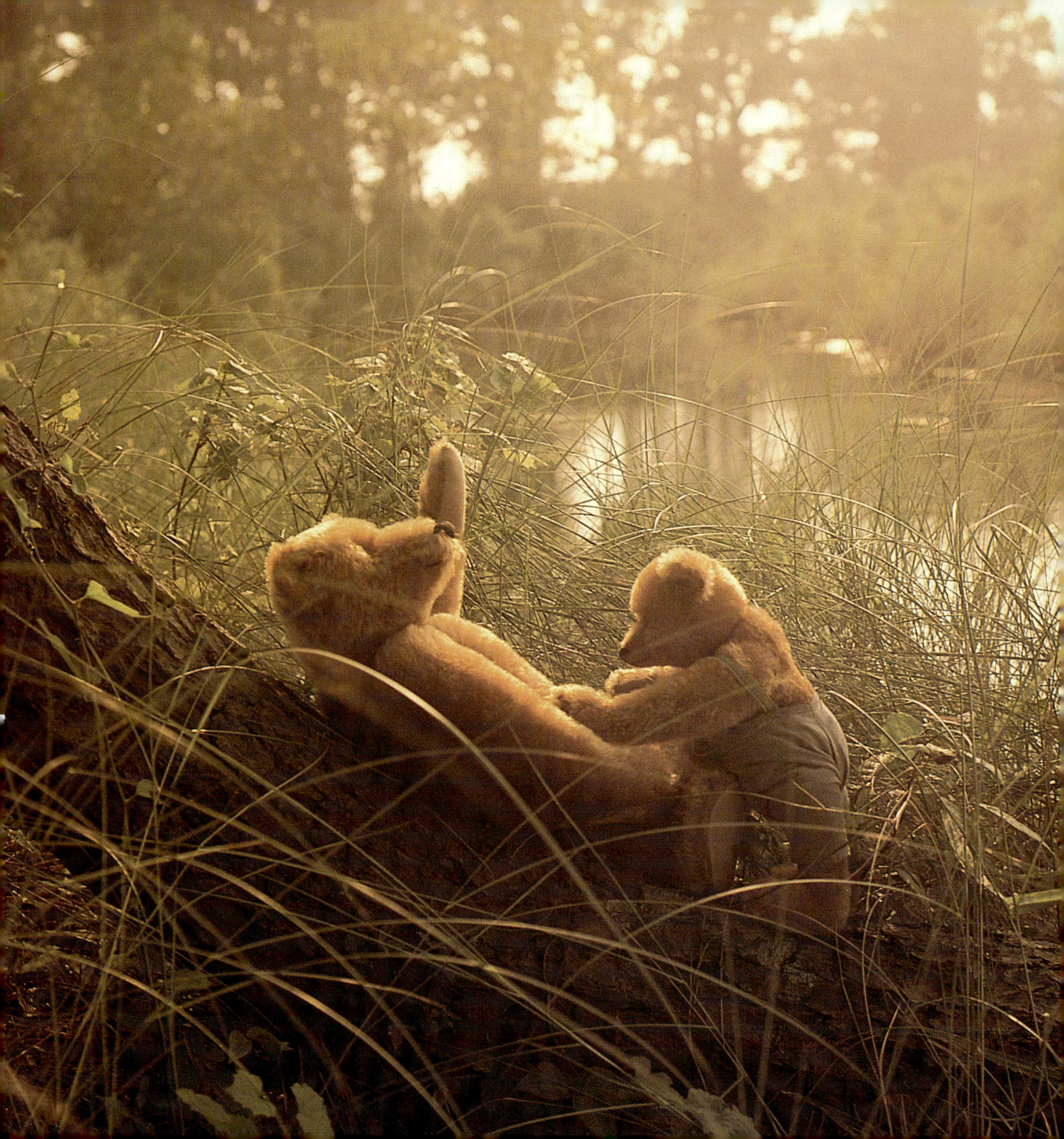

I saw two bears
Down by the river,
Sitting on a log,
Surrounded by a frog,
They played and layed,
And sang silly songs,
Down by the river bay.

Anna Wagenhals

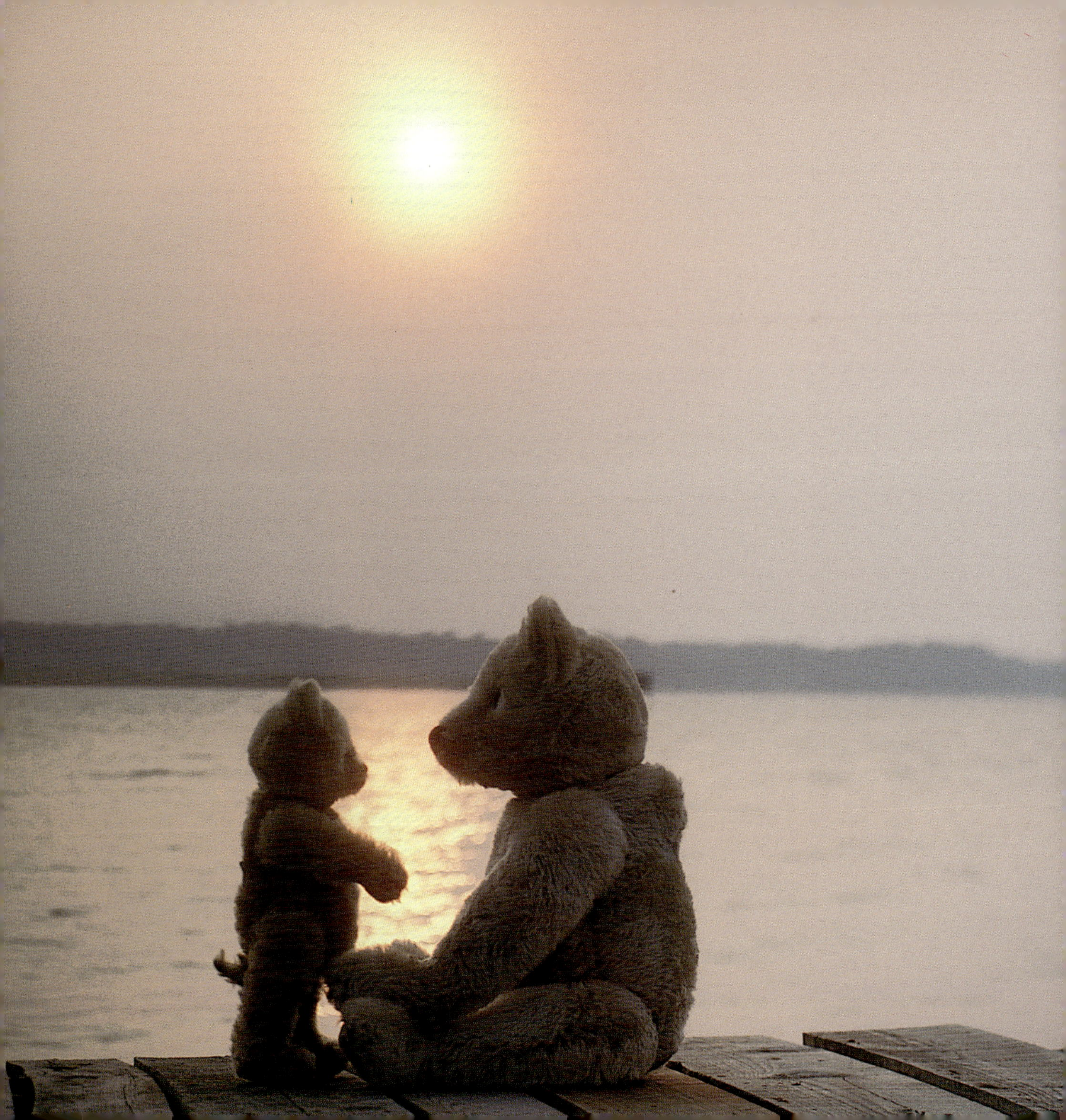

"Can I say something
to you, Mommy?"
Little Bear gently asked.
"Come closer and whisper
sweetly to me,
Little One,"
Mama Bear softly said.
"I love you, Mommy!"
"I love you too, Baby."

Ho Phi Le

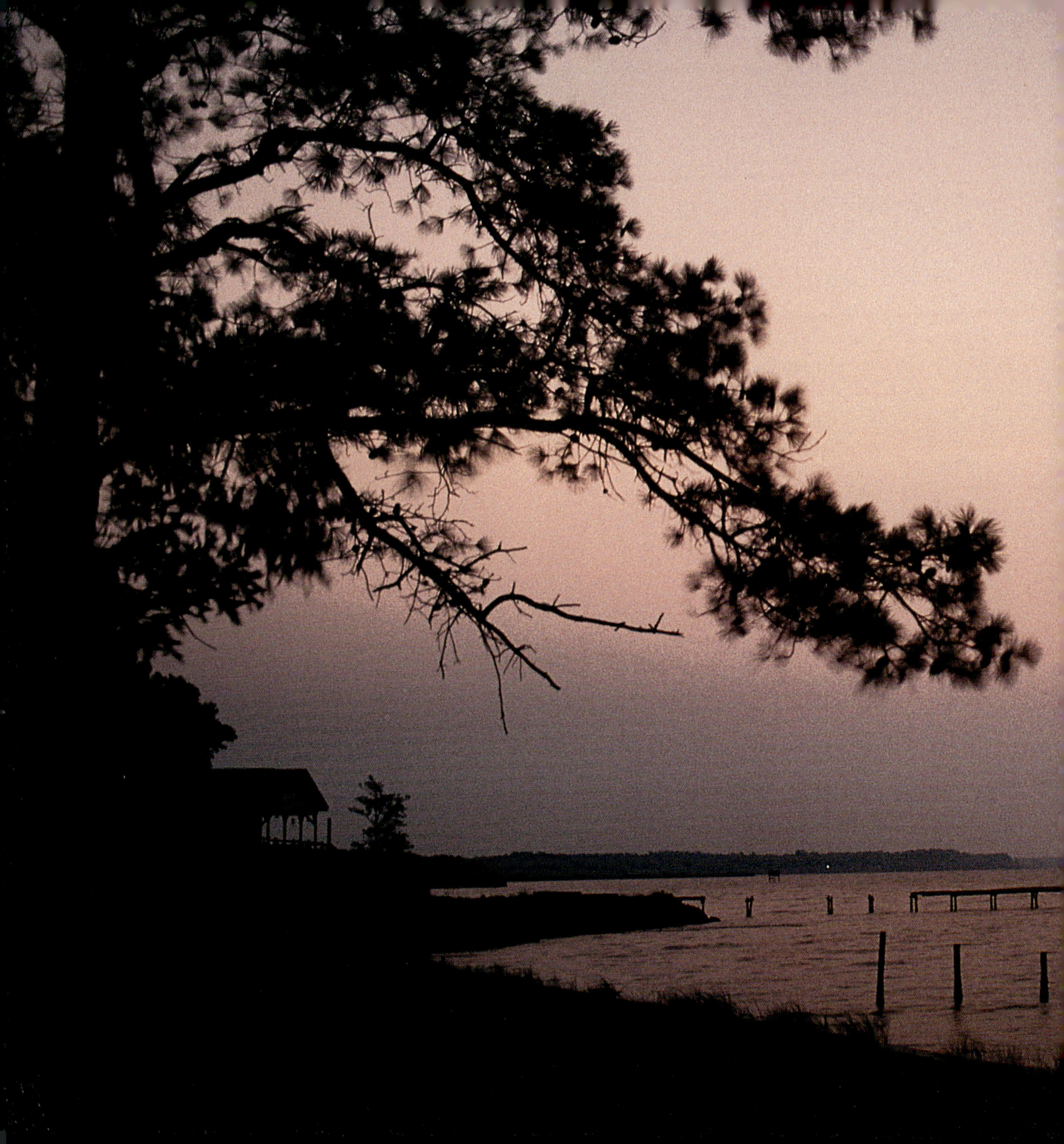

When the sun sets,
It's time to go to bed,
Sweet dreams, sweet dreams...baby,
Good night, good night...sweetie,
See you in the morning light...honey.

Ho Phi Le

Friendship plays an important part in my life, and that's why I'm so grateful to my faithful friends who have always been there for me. To know that we all share a tender love for teddy bears makes this book more special than any others. Thank you for sharing, caring and loving. Even though we are so far apart, I want you to know that I'll always be with you...by heart.

Mary and Gary Ruddell, Carolyn Cook, Paul Hardin, Neil Jarger, David Miller, Darrell Wagner, Hazel Coons, Jim Sanders, Dottie Ayers, Michele Clise, Mimi Hiscox, Michael Josselman, Dolores Baker, Pam Lefkowitz, Pam Brunelle, Connie Junk, Jeanette Warner, Cindy Martin, Pat Moore, Dan Frost, Steve Guthrie, Ernie DeBay, Rosemary Volpi, Audie Sison, Dianne Anderson, Patti Jedler, M.J. McDonald, Tammy Blank and my editor Mary Beth Ruddell.

Many thanks to my friends who have shared their wonderful collections with all of us: Susan & John Wiley, Steve Estes, Barbara Lauver, Barbara & Byron Baldwin, Polly & Penny Zaneski, Linda & Wally Mullins, Nancy Sandberg, Anna Taccino, Carol Else.

To all the children who have touched my life through the years: Christopher Smith, Steven McLain, Eva Young, Jessica & Christopher Baldwin, Julia Whyel, William Jones, Susan Scott, Laura Cook, Michael Parnes, Jonathan Lee, Emily Musick, Korina Rodriguez, Slavik Denchik, Norma Morales, Crystal Anderson, Anna Wagenhals, Sara Fey, Kevin Day, Stephanie Niner, Nichole Atkinson, Kelly Cunningham, Amanda Richardson, Gabe Conant, Jeff Lim, Kelly Leach, Christina Olson, Evan Junk.

And to my beloved mother, father, sisters, brother, nieces & nephews, goddaughter and godson,

with all my love...